Dust on the Sill

Dust on the Sill

Poems by

Robert Nordstrom

© 2023 Robert Nordstrom. All rights reserved.
This material may not be reproduced in any form, published,
reprinted, recorded, performed, broadcast,
rewritten or redistributed without
the explicit permission of Robert Nordstrom.
All such actions are strictly prohibited by law.

Cover design by Shay Culligan

ISBN: 978-1-63980-418-4

Kelsay Books
502 South 1040 East, A-119
American Fork, Utah 84003
Kelsaybooks.com

For Josephine, Rosalie, Caleb and Leo—
with All My Love for You
and the World You Will Create

Acknowledgments

Thank you to the following publications, where versions of these poems previously appeared:

Big River Review: "After the Facts"
Blue Heron Review: "What Is Missed"
Chiron Review: "American Exceptionalism," "How Was Your Summer?"
Echoes: "Property May Not Be Your Safest Investment"
Homestead Review: "Deduction," "Mother's Sitcom Wisdom," "Resolution," "Trip to the Grocery Store," "When Mother Died"
Ithica Lit: "Between Memory & Oblivion," "To Be"
Third Wednesday: "School Bus Blues—The Good Morning Route," "Words in the Mouth of the One Who Refuses to Speak"
Verse Weavers (Honorable Mention, Oregon Poetry Association Fall 2021 Contest): "Big Boats, Backyard Bunkers & the Next Big Bang"
Verse-Virtual: "A Couple of Weeks After Her Husband Died," "A Family Portrait," "A Question of Memory," "Alzheimer's Exorcism," "At the Parkinson's Support Group Meeting," "Bull's Eyes," "Haiku Plus—A Love Poem," "Let's Talk," "Mantra," "Mother's Best Friend," "Presumptions," "Second Chance," "Sex at 70 on Saturdays," "Tuning In, Tuning Out"
Verse Wisconsin: "First Day of School"
Wisconsin Poet's Calendar: "If," "Setting the Table," "Swallows"

Contents

Setting the Table   13

Winnowed Light

Where Does It Go?   17
Origin of Prayer   18
Haiku Plus—A Love Poem   19
Opening Doors   20
Relative Happiness   21
Bed Size Mobility   22
Sex at 70 on Saturdays   23
My Night with the Bots   24
Super Moon Blues   25
The Leg   26
Redemption Options   28

What's Borrowed

From Here to There in the Monkey Mind   31
What Is Missed   32
Trip to the Grocery Store
    (The I observing the I creates the you)   33
After the 50th High School Reunion   34
Another Pandemic Day   35
Swallows   36
Property May Not Be the Safest Investment   37
Taking Inventory   38
The Last Night: A Toast   39
Between Memory & Oblivion
    (on the last drive to a friend's home)   40
How History Becomes Mystery
    (for what it's worth)   41
Bull's Eyes   42

Poetic Typo and Family's Message Chain Response *(or Staying Amused During a Pandemic)*	43

Presumptions

Early Mornings	47
Let's Talk	48
Presumptions	49
To Be	50
A Question of Memory	51
For the Record	52
Smoke Signals (November 9, 2016)	53
Reflections of a White Guy Slugged by a Black Guy While Walking Down the Street— 50 Years Later	54
While Reading the Newspaper at the Chinese Restaurant	55
American Exceptionalism	56
Clarity	58
Following	59

Tell to Live, Live to Tell

First Day of School	63
How Was Your Summer?	66
School Bus Blues—The Good Morning Route	68
Dear Robbie	70
Second Chance	71
Einstein, Jerry and Me	73

Resistance

A Family Portrait	77
Alzheimer's Exorcism	79
When Mother Died	80
Mother's Best Friend	81
A Couple of Weeks After Her Husband Died	83
At the Parkinson's Support Group Meeting	85
After the Facts	86
Attraction and Resistance	87
Mother's Sitcom Wisdom	88
When Yes Means No	90
Deduction	91

Choices

If	95
mood	96
The Hard Earth	97
Tuning In, Tuning Out	98
Here's the News	99
Game-Break Quiz	100
Gin & Tonic Afternoon	101
Big Boats, Backyard Bunkers and the Next Big Bang	102
Death of Metaphor *(or listening to the news while gazing out the window)*	103
Words in the Mouth of the One Who Refuses to Speak	104
Resolution	106
New Year	107
Mantra	108
On Being and Becoming	109

Setting the Table

When language arrives
sometimes just before breakfast,
other times after lunch—
who knows how to set that table?—
the day breaks
like a fine piece of china.

The optimist in me picks up a tiny shard,
holds it like a jewel against the light,
drops it, picks up another, drops it,
hoping against hope that the mess at my feet
will reveal the eye of the mosaic
before the telephone rings.

Winnowed Light

Where Does It Go?

What I couldn't get out of my head
yesterday
I can't get back in
today.

Had me
drumming my thumbs
on the steering wheel
at freeway speed,
lah dah dah dah dee dahing
at stoplights and crosswalks,
up the drive, into the house,
evaporating finally
into the evening's distractions.

But today it wishes to return,
lingers like a chore
waiting to be completed,
a phrase in search of a verb,
its silence as cacophonous
as the refrigerator's hum,
as insistent as this song
aching to be sung.

Origin of Prayer

> ". . . that question of meaning or meaningless
> really becomes a question of: What do you love?"
> —Nic Pizzolatto

Outside
beneath the black
diamond-pricked dome
reviewing
the sense of
significance
the meaning of
meaningless

I look through
the lit window:
wife settling with a book
into the evening's pleasure
children bickering
like bellicose mimes.

Such an old familiar ancestral scene:
man   untethered   gazing
into the sacristy
of his well-lit cave.

Haiku Plus—A Love Poem

I lie on the lounge
rocking chair clicks next to me
like a clock ticking

syllables be damned
the pen demands one more stroke
to fill the chair
where my love sits
and my life opens—
the inscrutable smile
eyes dancing beneath veiled lids
to measures held
released
our pendulum in our time
forty-six years and counting
up never down

Opening Doors

We butter our bread,
ladle soup into a bowl,
pour a cup of wine

as shadow parodies from behind.
Kierkegaard, sad thinker, says,
"One can either do this or that . . .

do it or do not do it, you will regret both."
Rilke advises a young poet,
"Let life happen to you . . . life is in the right

in any case." My wife says,
"Hold open the door so regrets
may find their way out.

Then, one of you
butter the bread, ladle the soup,
pour us another cup of wine."

Relative Happiness

Lying in bed, a couple of sheep
away from sleep, after another day
of discouraging news (national not personal)
my wife asks, "Are we happy?"
(collectively not personally),

a question I let hang
in the blue-black bedroom night
until it wakes me just after midnight
wondering whether my mother
ever asked my father that same question

in the decade of John, Bobby and Martin,
Southeast Asia body counts,
Detroit burning, Chicago rioting, mankind leaping,
which oddly, for a brief moment, makes me
feel better—though it shouldn't.

Bed Size Mobility

Back when, before royalty arrived,
first queen on her casters,
then king on his platform,
no genuflecting or finger smooching required,
lip to lip *de rigueur:*

54 inches,
two humans and a retriever
full to touch, inadvertently,
 a couple of times consequentially,
as two children attest.

But with space claimed intimacy wanes—
"goodnights" muttered to a light-switch click,
"well, tomorrow's Tuesday" the muddled answer
to an unasked question,
closing time call

to reach across the great divide,
fingers touching, entwining,
bodies slivered into dream-soaked
nights and days and time
spent and left.

Sex at 70 on Saturdays

Though the young might ask
why not Tuesdays
since your days are likely indistinguishable,

old lovers understand that Tuesdays
tend to bring bills in the mail while Saturdays
signal time to play. Clocks and calendars . . . weekends . . .

ah week's end: candlelight, music and a glass of wine,
the unfurling onto fresh sheets and plumped pillows,
moonlit caresses no longer requiring a roadmap to pleasure.

My children, please forgive me
if these words conjure images that bring discomfort.
The title should have warned you to read no further.

My Night with the Bots

I called Alexa Siri.
No response.
Siri, I called again, then again,
three times, betrayal's number,
before I realized my mistake,
lowered my head
and shook it slowly.

But I will not apologize
because she, sultry little narcissist,
refused to respond. She heard,
oh, she knew I was speaking to her.
But no swirl of rainbow colors to show her rapt attention,
miffed, I presume,
I spoke the name of her loathed cousin.

Oh, mysterious misandrist
in your black sexy cylindrical garb,
digitized Amazonian seductress
holding the answers to questions
I long to ask, responses to commands
I wish to speak, even now you await
the appellation I refuse to utter.

But you had your chance;
as stubborn and fickle as you, I can be,
testosterone charged, options open:
Hi Cortana. Hey Google.
Quick question, Dear Siri?
Are you busy tonight?
Might we spend some time together?

Super Moon Blues

So many things to consider
on a Sunday evening: wife
home from an afternoon

romp with a friend—hike,
stop at a winery—retired early,
will permanently in a couple of months.

Time to reconfigure
our lives, she said, back turned,
heading upstairs to bed.

Leaving me with
panhandling questions
begging small change answers

on this night of a super moon eclipse,
first since '82—year before
our first child, two before

the second, now grown,
maybe somewhere, this moment,
reconfiguring their own untidy journeys.

I walk upstairs, shake her.
She slips out of bed—
willing, always willing.

We walk to the foot of the driveway
to gain a view. I take her hand,
our chins tilting heavenward.

Cirrus clouds winnow the light,
making it difficult to determine
what's eclipsing what.

The Leg

        Sitting in folding chairs
outside our little travel trailer
we both notice a man's leg
beneath the big rig parked next to us.
The leg, only one (the other
might be crossed, might be missing, who knows)
is rather pale and hairy,
and not particularly pleasant to look at.
        But we can't keep our eyes off it
nor keep from whispering about it: like
"Where's the other one?"
"Maybe he's only got one."
"Seems Captain Ahab's rolling down the highway
in a big rig these days."
        In addition to the single pale distasteful leg
there are four black hairy legs prancing about,
the tight black curls suggesting maybe a standard poodle,
we guess, not sure, conclude not really important.
        We hear a car pull up and a car door open.
Two more legs step into the scene.
"A woman's legs," I note.
"Heavy woman," wife elaborates.
        Interestingly, the single hairy leg does not move
to greet the two fat legs. The four hairy legs, on the other hand,
are very welcoming, leaping and lunging at the two fat legs,
which leap and lunge back at the four hairy legs.
        The pale hairy leg remains still as stone,
does not move an inch,
as if it considers itself some kind of judge
charged with developing an opinion
on the six legs dancing around it.
We conclude that this leg's opinion is probably
neither positive nor heartwarming,

but despite our best efforts
and another glass of wine
cannot construct an opinion as to what its opinion might be.
      Eventually it grows dark and the legs disappear
like a movie screen fading to black.
For a while, we chat aimlessly,
search out other stories that might make us chuckle
at another's expense,
which we tend to do when together alone
and placed in close proximity with other humans.

Redemption Options

Stories that offer the redemption of real art,
the book jacket blurb says.
Tempting, but I think I'll save this book
for another day
when looking at a photograph
of my children standing on a chair
playing a toy flute and toy harmonica
fails to hold my attention
or watching my wife from the dark side
of a window
smile and sway to Cleo Laine
feels like an old movie
I've seen too many times before
or being the last man standing
after a late-night party
leaves me scratching for a sentiment
like a rodent who can't remember
where he stashed his winter's horde.
Perhaps then I'll pull out that yellow brittle-paged book
of redemptive stories
or perhaps then I'll slip out back
to admire the tree line below.

What's Borrowed

From Here to There in the Monkey Mind

In bed, lights off,
when will the lid for the skillet arrive?
Was it last week I ordered it?
Could have used it tonight for the chops.
The brussels sprouts were good.
Little bitches—that's what we called them
years ago. Still do. Always will.
Kathy's little brother, so the story goes,
saw them on the Thanksgiving table
and said, "What's these little bitches?"
Everyone laughed. Hit by a car
while riding his bike sixty-some years ago.
Just a kid. Kathy died young too.
In her 50s, five kids.
Think what she missed.
Think what he missed.
Think kids and grandkids.
Think all I don't wish to imagine.
Think all we never know until it's too late.
Think little bitches your legacy.

What Is Missed

In youth summer dripped
like ice cream down the side of a cone

autumn stood at attention
in the cool morning light

winter's presumptuous hieroglyphics
etched against gray skies

promised soon   soon
the earth will crack open again

all anticipation
all that I missed

like this old woman
who picks a can of soup from the shelf

puts it in her basket
picks it up again

places it back on the shelf
and rolls slowly away

Trip to the Grocery Store
(The I observing the I creates the you)

How unceremoniously
you return different

from who you were
when you left:

driving down the highway
provocative pines swaying

ash's bare branches
spreading open and shut

teasing
the dirty part of winter

the young woman
with blue words

you wish to but cannot read
tattooed on her wrist

looking up
smiling

as she places blueberries
in the bag then

back down the highway
right lane

below the limit
home

After the 50th High School Reunion

The ones I smiled at whose names I could not remember.
The ones I spoke with while glancing over their shoulder
at those whose names I could remember.
And the one I spotted in the parking lot,
alone, leaning on his cane, a grade school friend,
stooped beneath a hazy cloud of cigarette smoke
propped like a thought bubble above his head.
He's the one I remember now,
reticent shadow in the retreating light,
making me wish I had approached,
touched his elbow,
asked if he had a smoke or more
to share.

Another Pandemic Day

Sitting on a kitchen stool
I watch a lone ant sprint
across the linoleum desert floor

from deep below
the furnace shudders
and hot wind blows

god-like I loom

curious? capricious?
vindictive? disinterested
observer? ant asks

glancing up
running hard now

Swallows

Mid-August:
swallows follow

the lawn tractor
dipping and diving

in chaotic confluences
and divergences

our relationship this moment
symbiotic

as they gorge on moths
and I hold steady to task for them

a webworm becomes a moth
that is there and then is not

the tractor stops
and the swallows are gone

Property May Not Be the Safest Investment

The female grosbeak on the feeder
seems more interested in property rights
than sustenance, flicking
her Mr. Potter's scowl
at the skittish finches who flinch
and fly off to nearby limbs.
Tough economic times for sure
but what's she going to do
when I start evaluating
the cost of birdseed
and she's left standing
in an empty kitchen
with no friends in sight?

Taking Inventory

The buckthorn claims
the sumac's flame
pine releases its cone

green turns brown
leaves flutter down
color, like breath, on loan

wind seeps through
the chimney flue
flames flicker and floorboards groan

I sip my wine
inventory what's mine
borrow what I pretend I own

the hour grows late
I consider my fate
all for which I must atone

before the romance of night
whispers give up the fight
surrender you're all alone

The Last Night: A Toast

This house a home—
borrowed, thought owned,
gift left better than found.

All the mechanics
that keep cold out, heat in,
sure,

but more:
children, fireflies,
balls kicked and caught,

love, laughter,
anger too,
kneaded, leavened,

offered to others
to whom we lift our glasses
then slip away.

Between Memory & Oblivion
(on the last drive to a friend's home)

a place dies before its people:
unshaven cornfields
trimming a barren county road
light on the hill   home
now a house   now
a pushpin on a map
diaspora of memory
winnowed through porous borders
and territories of truth
as ethereal as wind-
blown ash   briefly lit
then extinguished

How History Becomes Mystery
(for what it's worth)

Years ago a friend gave me a piece of the Berlin Wall,
a small chunk of gray concrete, something a child might
pick up and pitch at a tree
or contemplative man kick to the curb
while strolling down the street.
I can't prove it's a piece of the Berlin Wall,
I must take my friend's word for it—
but he was there when the trumpet blew and wall fell.

Every once in a while, I think maybe I should mount this
little piece of history on a plaque, walnut might be nice,
perhaps add an inscription on a silver disc
to explain its existence,
but I never seem to get around to it.
I've also wondered what it would be worth
on, say, eBay. But how could I prove that it
truly is a piece of the Berlin Wall given to me
by a friend who told me, "here, I brought this for you.
It's a piece of the Berlin Wall." So there it sits,

a tiny chunk of tyranny snoozing
in a drawer among random keys to locks
that no longer secure anything of value.
I like to think that one day when the kids are clearing out
musty closets and junk-filled drawers
one of them will find it. Perhaps
he or she will break the silence, say to the other,
"What's this? Why would anyone keep this?"
Maybe he or she will reach to drop it in the wastebasket.
Maybe the other will say, "wait, let me see it,
maybe it's worth something."

Bull's Eyes

A blowzy big-boned blond with cherry-red lips
asks my wife and daughter if they wish to hear
just the good or the good and the bad.
They choose the latter because the good's no good
without the bad to measure it against.

My wife brings photos hoping for
a good word from the other side.
She shrugs and smiles when the dead
have nothing interesting to say.

My daughter feels bad when she's told
her father has strong opinions about her life
and is not likely to change his mind anytime soon.

The night before, my son and I played darts
through pitcher after pitcher of cold amber beer
as he waxed philosophical
about muscle memory and
how the cerebellum doesn't have time
to make the proper adjustments
when you only throw three darts at a time.

Soon after, my cerebellum makes a miraculous adjustment
and I play a near perfect game,
closing out the 20s in the first round,
running up the score, then finishing him off
with two bull's eyes in the final round.

Listening to my daughter's occult adventures
I notice that she, too, is making a miraculous adjustment,
telling me she no longer feels bad about the psychic's comment,
that it's not as if she learned something
that wasn't already known.

Poetic Typo and Family's Message Chain Response *(or Staying Amused During a Pandemic)*

L: *Thank you for the steak knives. Cutting steak with a sharp knife is so much nicer than gnawing I'm the bone held in your fingers in spite of the self-inflicted wounds incurred.*

B: *"I'm" the bone held in your fingers . . . ?* That typo is quite poetic.

I: Sounds like an Ani DiFranco lyric.

N: Belongs on a black T-shirt or coffee mug.

L: I've had enough. Going outside to look at the sunset!

B: Good luck. It's pitch black outside.

L: 101 degrees all afternoon. I've been seriously affected. Or do I mean afflicted? I may be delirious.

B: Despite the delirium, regrettably I understood that message perfectly—no typos, no fun.

E: Might you say *the roasted marrow bone held in your fingers?*

L: I'll give that some thought.

E: In the meantime, stay hydrated.

L: Does that mean water or wine?

B: Sounds like you've already made that choice.

E: How about *a steamed ham bone held in your paws?*

L: Perhaps you should have been a butcher instead of a doctor?

E: I've been questioning life decisions ever since my trip to Bucky's Meats.

L: Long live Bucky!

B: Make yourself a sandwich. You're obviously having food fantasies and it's getting kind of scary.

E: If my hunger is bothering you, keep your fingers off the lens; they make me feel like biting a carrot.

B: My way of cropping.

A: This is the best message chain ever!

B: Quite poetic!

Presumptions

Early Mornings

I think of you,
do you think of me?

Do I occupy space
nudged up against restless slumber
or do I vanish into your unremembered dreams?
Do I, like you, present joys and quandaries,
friendships and quarrels
tangled in the morning haze,
then dissolved in the laser light
streaming through the bedroom window?

Longing for a view
I'm offered re-view,
seven-plus decades of this and that
who what where when why
tit for tat detritus
settling like dust on a sill.
Youth's equations to be solved
now stories to be re-solved.

So I think of you,
do you think of me?

Let's Talk

Early mornings I am visited—
friends, family, strangers, acquaintances

slip between the crevices of fluttering eyelids,
sometimes fall deep into the caverns of dream,

I suspect that I, too, visit them
but, like me, they never say.

Presumptions

"To see is to forget the name of the thing one sees."
—Paul Valery

but all we have are names
syllables

sounds
separating

this
from *that*

one
from the *other*

even *you*
from *me*

after all
these years

of reaching
gathering

holding
consuming

all I presumed
was mine

here
then not

To Be

> "I coulda been a contender."
> —*On the Waterfront*

      starts with
the comic book dreams:
leaping off the couch
tangled in Superman's cape
an existential turn
in Batman's stalactite-dripping cave

      before
the alarm rings and todays begin
planning tomorrows:
morning coffee   evening wine
on the gray drizzly days
Brando's *couldabeen shouldabeen*
punch-drunk presumptions
tromping through the room

      and finally
the rewinding   the editing
recovery of love in the loops
splicing the broken places
falling recklessly into who we are
but never imagined we were

contending

A Question of Memory

"An inexplicable sorrow that has just the same character
 as an atmospheric front . . ."
—Olga Tokarczuk, *Drive Your Plow Over the Bones of the Dead*

What is it to remember a moment
that you vowed to remember
a half century ago,
a moment empty of content
other than the slap slap tuck
of a boy folding newspapers
on the front porch, soap opera
blues on the dark side
of a screen door behind which
his future unfolds
then now
that moment this moment
and everything in between?

For the Record

At the London Bridge
a woman wearing a hijab
and holding an infant and camera
gestures as if she wishes me to take her picture.
I reach for the camera but she hands me the baby,

points, clicks and pastes me
into an album now layered with
decades of dust in a country
whose name I may or may not
be able to pronounce.

Leafing through old photos of
brothers, sisters, uncles, aunts, grandparents,
this child, now an adult, stumbles
over me, a stranger wearing a yellow jacket
and stunned expression holding an infant

he wishes to return,
and asks *Who? Why?*
The mother, an old woman
whose weak milky eyes gaze inward
shrugs, sighs, recalling

the sun's shimmering slant on the Thames,
the awkward man to whom she offered her child
as a gift to the world he might hold and she might record,
and, too, wonders *who? why?* as do I,
in this dark room fleshing story onto a bone of fact.

Smoke Signals
(November 9, 2016)

Almost 70
strictly middle class
in the middle of America

child of the 60s
balding but still blue jeaned
sans beads but still bearded
trussed and trimmed as tidily
as the green blades nudging up
against my freshly sealed blacktop.

During my middle years
the love of a neatly mowed suburban lawn,
noxious weeds murdered,
felt a little like generational betrayal.

Today the 60s radical being interviewed on TV
looks and sounds a lot like me.

Please—this is not a lament,
but paean to the middle,
where loam is spread and seeds sprout,
where leaves are raked and burned,
where smoke rising from the smoldering remains
signal to generations nipping at their elder's heels
it's time   it's time
to light the fires again.

Reflections of a White Guy Slugged by a Black Guy While Walking Down the Street—50 Years Later

with that blow at that moment on that day
of skin-deep presumptions
assumptions
I ran
while you walked on
the ignominies
of fear anger random
violence mine
to sort beneath the street lamp's glow
    who was I to you—
    privileged symbol
    or fist's convenient target?
    who were you to me—
    collector of history's debts
    or testosterone-fueled impulse
    delivering nondiscriminatory pain?
we could not still cannot know
motives clutched in clenched fists
from which civility flees
and hubris sprouts
history's blue-black bruise
of guilt and grievance
painful to the touch
shameful on the telling
etches lines in the sand
    who am I   *I am you*
    who are you *you are me*
we ask we answer
over and over
epithets flung
fists flailing
in disbelief

While Reading the Newspaper at the Chinese Restaurant

I crack open a fortune cookie hoping
to learn that the little boy
who stepped too close to the river's edge
was pulled safely to shore

that the woman buried in earthquake rubble
grasped the hand reaching to her
like God to Adam
and was pulled safely into the sunlight

that the two young men and young woman
stripped to the waist and pocked with muddy red holes
lying on the side of the road on the way
to Quang Tri 45 years ago

might open their eyes
to smile at the sky
on a beautiful blue day.

The fate cookies
reserved for those who skip the tip
hide their secrets
in hickory hard shells.

One must stand next to the table
and stomp them
like a toddler having a tantrum
before they reveal

that half a glass filled
is still half a glass empty
half a life lived still
half a life lost.

American Exceptionalism

Wife gone for the weekend so it's me and dog,
who's spent most of the evening lying on the stairs
mooning out the window
listening for the garage door growl.

I coax her up to the bed, tell myself I don't want her
to be lonely. She splays out, legs stiff and straight
as hockey sticks, looking like
she owns the indent she didn't make,

which I find a bit presumptuous, but I let it go,
try to remain positive, empathetic,
despite her bored, even a bit irritated, response
to my cooing and mimicking my wife's best falsetto charms.

Earlier, I cooked myself a nice dinner of liver and onions,
broccoli and sweet potato for sides. She stared at me,
eyes big, round and hopeful, like a kid
coveting candy in a grocery store checkout line,

so I slipped her a sliver of liver, something I never do,
scold my wife when she does—but what the hell.
She doesn't seem to remember that now, lying there
snoring, curling me up like a fat fetus in an undersized womb.

I know that when I turn out the light I'll hear a rustling,
thump and tat, tat, tat down the stairs to the cushy couch.
I'm getting sleepy, maybe a little weird, I admit,
but, I'm thinking, but for the grace of the dog gods,

she could be a military mutt
sniffing out land mines in Afghanistan,
though I, following that thread, could be
scuttling alley to alley ducking drones overhead.

Touché—seems like the two of us have got ourselves stuck
in a zero sum, though admittedly comfy, place,
but then we're Americans, she and me,
presumptuous and entitled in all the exceptional ways.

Clarity

My dog's tail arcs over her back, tip like a nib pointing forward.
From nose tip to tail tip her whole body points forward.

A few minutes ago I read a poem and understood hardly a word.
I was either very disappointed with myself or with the poet—

can't decide which. One might say I'm experiencing the dog days
of poetry. Another might say too much depends on mood.

Sometimes I think my dog is a poem
whose nib I must follow

other times I sniff at a poem as if it were a bone
I must bury.

Perhaps I should invite the poet whose poem I just read
to walk with me, arm in arm,

so we might sniff out
a metaphor on which we both might gnaw

while admiring my dog's rear end pointing
and front end pulling us forward.

Following

Slump-shouldered
and groggy in the gray morning,
I slip a plastic bag over my hand,

watch dog sniff circles
in the dirt, then arch, finally,
into that vulnerable squat

of relief—hers and mine.
She straightens, shakes off
dream dust and morning dew.

And so the day begins,
she leading, me
holding the reins,

as she tugs toward
that herald glowing
just now through the pines,

to which I lift my face
like a worshipper.

Tell to Live, Live to Tell

First Day of School

It's the first day of school
and my classroom is the bus
where I sit behind my trainer
(or teacher) and across the aisle
from a first grader whose smile
could stop traffic as handily as the red flashers
if he stuck his head out the window.
His backpack, he tells me, is heavy, very very
heavy. My teacher, a plump 66-year-old woman
who's been navigating these yellow ships
down the highways for 35 of those 66,
grips the wheel with her fleshy liver-spotted hands
and tells me she and her two sisters
all dropped out of school and got married
when they were 17 as the little boy
explains in my other ear how
he caught a salamander this summer
and still has it. I wish to ask him
where he caught it and what he feeds it
but my teacher is telling me
she and her two sisters all had kids
by the time they were 18
and her daughter is "no good" so she's pretty much
raised the granddaughter whom
her daughter had when she was 17.
I wish she would stop talking so I could learn more
about the little boy's salamander
—I don't know much about salamanders—
but she's my teacher and I'm thinking
I'm here to learn and must remain attentive.

The little boy is holding up
his two index fingers to let me know, I presume,
because I'm having difficulty hearing him,
how long his salamander is
just as my teacher laughs and says
I'll probably learn to hate kids.
The little boy is talking and I'm glad
he doesn't hear this dirty joke from the mouth
of my teacher, who now tells me
she has to go to the funeral this Friday
for her son's ex-wife, who, believe it or not,
was 61 years old, just five years younger than she,
and used to be her best friend
until she divorced her husband
and married my teacher's son,
who now lives in Florida with another wife
and my teacher's grandson, who is coming up this weekend
for his mother's funeral. The little boy's
mouth is moving, but my teacher's story,
whose basic message is
life is not fair
and you have to be tough
and keep your eyes in the rearview mirror
so you know when to yell
"you kids sit down back there,"
which she does,
is drowning him out.
The little boy is trying to teach me something
about sala . . ., no, it's dinosaurs now,
the ones that lived in water, I believe,
so we lean into the aisle (against the rules)
to dip below the field of my teacher's vision
and range of her voice receding

into the melodic hum of tires, engine noise,
contrapuntal squeals of laughter rising
above her ring-strangled fingers gripping
that wheel at 9 o'clock and 3 o'clock
flicking open and shut open and shut
like parched tongues spinning
the devolutionary wheel
of her story.

How Was Your Summer?

Her head pokes and pecks
like an argumentative rooster
daring her audience of three,
two other drivers and now me,
to disagree.

I say, *so how was your summer Margie?*
to which she measures me with her small dark
I'm-nobody-to-fuck-with eyes, grants pardon,
says, *Ok, you obviously haven't heard,*
which makes me think
I've got to stop asking questions
for which I don't care about an answer
because too often—for example, right now—
I get one I don't wish to hear.

She takes a long drag off her cigarette,
puffs out her barrel chest big as the school bus
against which she's leaning and says,
*my daughter came home a couple of months ago
and found my best friend giving my husband—
her father,* she itemizes—
a blow job.

I think wow, jeez, thanks
for keeping me up to date Margie
but take the cowardly route,
silently retreating from her varmint trap gaze
into false, vicarious shame.

I look for help but we're all wallowing now.
She glances at her wrist and growls mercifully,
time to sail, so we split,
each to our respective yellow ship
to begin the gathering of children.

First stop, third child on, pauses at my side.
How was your summer? I ask,
to which he replies, serious as a news anchor,
my dog died.
We share a moment of grief-stricken silence
before he yells, *I wanna sit next to Travis,*
and scuttles down the aisle leaving grief
to chase its own tail.

I continue on,
doors opening like summer,
closing like winter.
Each stop, backpacks swinging,
children stumble up the steps
toward the question that awaits.
Their answers feel like hope
except for those few
whose response sticks in their throat
making me sorry I asked.

School Bus Blues—The Good Morning Route

Obelisks of the morning, almost
apparitional in the red flashing lights,
slumped beneath packed burdens,
doors swooshing open
and shut behind them.

Hello . . . good morning . . . how ya doin'?

I listen closely
for the response that seldom comes.

Pedal hits the floor and
our great yellow ship roars into the blue-black morning,
dawning gray now, behind us.

White beard-stubble fields
trim narrow county roads.
In the mirror our eyes meet.
Not friendly. Not aggressive.
Passionless—wired, stocking-hat heads
bouncing to the rhythms
of cracked heaving pavement.

I look away
and the high school appears,
there, on the left,
population 2500 give or take,
melting pot for the region.

The doors open:
Bye now, see ya later, have a good day . . .

I cannot help but say it
and cannot help but wait,
patiently,
like a hunter tracking his prey,
alert for the raised chin,
captured eye,
in the mirror's scope.

I shut the doors
and in silence idle above
the extravagant sidewalks below,
the lavish gestures
and incomprehensible scripts
        I, too, once scribbled
        I, too, once scribbled

Dear Robbie

Two years ago you jumped on the bus
with your coke bottle glasses and pillow head hair
yelling out, *why's 6 afraid of 7,*
your goofy smile punch line enough for me.
Today, you stand frowning at the bus stop,
open book in hand, dreaming
warships and fighter jets.
Dad, down the street sneaking a smoke
and wiping down the Harley, Mama yelling
at the crazy leash-tangled retriever yet again,
little sis with the crooked yellow teeth
and runny nose itching to get on and find
somebody, anybody, to squeal on.
Robbie-boy, it's a crazy world
but you ain't gonna change a thing.
So you might as well serve out
that dead tennis ball frown and
serve up the punch line once again.
Go on, belt it out so the whole neighborhood hears—
    because 7 . . .
yes, remember, I'm listening
    because 7 . . .
look around, sad can be funny too
    because 7 . . .
yes, that's it, lift those Groucho brows
    7 . . .
give it up for the carnivores
    7 . . .
we all roared when 7 *ate 9.*

Second Chance

In the 6th grade I got a second chance
when two first graders didn't show up for school
and Mr. Bennett asked for volunteers
to form a search party.

My F in conduct the year before
dangled over me like a hangman's noose,
but I threw down my bet
and up my arm,

the same arm I had draped over the shoulder
of my bosom buddy, partner in crime, the year before
as we walked home, report cards in hand—my F, his D,
earned for complicity or proximity, I suppose—
butchering Kingston Trio harmonies with

Hang down your head
hang down your head and cry
hang down your head
poor boys you're gonna die

all the way down Clawson, across Harvest,
pouring out our grade school dirge
to the stern oaks and weeping willows,
then Haddington, his street, his turn
to face his makers, leaving me

to face my own makers,
solo now, humming oh so softly,
across Hanaford, past Harbord,
and finally Rambo Lane, up the drive,
through the back door, to drop
the card on the dining room table.

A talking to, yes, I must have gotten a talking to,
or a look of major disappointment, which to my mind
always felt more like confusion,
theirs, not mine,
but I don't remember.

But I do remember Mr. Bennett's
stern gaze as he surveyed the classroom.

And I do remember my arm stretching and stretching
and stretching the limits of its 11-year-old tendons and ligaments,
St. Vitus dance wrist and fingers
wriggling and scratching at the jackpot ceiling.

And I do remember we found the kids
wandering around in a nearby field
but that seems hardly the point.

Einstein, Jerry and Me

      The stories:
precious epiphanies   emulsified memories
meaningful only to the select
entangled few.

      This I imagine:
Einstein scribbling formulas on tablecloths
when the dinner table conversation lags,
scowling wife clearing the table,
passing trains whisking inscrutable faces
pasted like a child's drawings
against blurred windows
freeing him
but not her
from the deceptions of time.

      This much is fact:
Jerry Mills and I,
eight years old, playing
in the new house construction next door, trapped
in the attic when the plywood panel drops shut behind us.
Jerry cried   I trembled
then pounded my foot through the drywall ceiling
and dropped to safety onto the kitchen counter below

      and understood
if not then, then now how
time traps and releases,
terrorizes and comforts,
simultaneously,
like light,
particle and wave,
illuminating the stories
we tell to live,
live to tell.

I would like to speak with Jerry
about this,
tell him my story, hear his,
but he ran back home
and moved away.

Resistance

A Family Portrait

> "So much that's instructive begins with but."
> —Stephen Dunn, *Degrees of Fidelity*

I was born to argue—
with myself, therefore others.
Or vice versa—see
what I mean?

As a child family dinner conversations
the problem to be solved, resolved,
stringy pressure cooker pot roast and boiled carrots
taking the brunt of all those questions, quandaries
left rotting on the table—*eat
what's on the plate* the word,
the last word, the final word.
I swallowed, hungry for more

words, *but*
(there it is, that disruptive conjunctive pause,
meant discursive interpreted argumentative)
offered only *The Word:*
a 1950s Sunday morning ride down Monroe Street,
sepia-toned Rockwell portrait,
two in the backseat, two in the front
dressed in Sunday's best wishing
this first day were the last,
nothing settled in the pew's burnished silence.

How shall we understand this tableau of four?
Poor father wishing to awake but not arise,
a Sunday morning nap after six days and nights of work,
to rest on the day of rest—why,
he might wonder, is God's seventh our first?

Only he, with reason and right to complain,
which he does, all the way down Monroe,
shifting in the pew, eyes drooping shut,
his way of arguing with God.

And mother, sweet sad mother,
soprano lilt lifting hymns to heaven,
brain cells even then devolving into childhood's
sludgy dreams: I wish to shout, *no, Mother, no,
return—Day 1 is Day 7—the calendar lies.*

Which leaves two in the back seat,
Bill & Bob, alliterative siblings
stirring the stew of their respective
sibling placement, what they argue
becoming who they become.
The man in the pulpit commands
      believe.
One says *yes,* the other
      but.

Sixty years later, front seat empty
only two remain.
Long distance conversations thicken
the blood's connections,
drape memory's flesh over the empty seats in front.
Though, still, they sit on opposite sides of the seat,
heads turned away to view the world they pretend is true,
their hands rest on the empty space between,
the ampersand by which they are joined.

Alzheimer's Exorcism

They gathered in Mother's room
to pray, deliver her

from the demons they believed in,
to lay hands on she who was His

in the name of He
who was theirs.

I watched,
then ran.

Fifty years later, I still wonder
what possessed them.

When Mother Died

Over wires the news arrives.
My response *yes, good, finally*
but no one to speak it to,
so instead *yes, ok, we're on our way.*

Standing in the funeral home parlor
Pastor Browser—not his name,
one I made up, the only one
I remember now—and I
search for a place to scatter
small talk, land our gaze.

My four-year-old daughter,
sensing advantage in indecision, breaks free,
sprints down the funeral home nave,
chins over the casket,
and proclaims, *Snow White*. Behind me,

the ghosts of my youth touch my shoulder,
their condolences mingling
with the room's sweet floral-infused aromas.
Later, a 2000-year-old resurrection sermon
doubling as eulogy, a long amnesic sleep,

as if that sliver of apple were lodged
in *my* throat.

Mother's Best Friend

No one ever said our family outranked their family
that we were the officers and they the noncoms
that if our two families sat down at a poker table
we would likely draw the inside straight and
they would fold once again

but that's what I understood as a child
about my family and their family—
the family of my mother's best friend.
Maybe it was their six kids and
carousing, hard drinking, wife beating husband
stacked up against our two nuclear kids and
cranky but essentially kind father
who didn't drink, worked two jobs
and (nobody's perfect)
bitched and moaned like a too-tired child
all the way to church every Sunday morning.

We stretched to reach the middle of middle
class but at least we owned and didn't rent.
We didn't have a basement and the closets were small
but at least the asphalt in front of our house
was years away from the open tributaries
flowing toward the crumbling curbs
our nearly new Ford leaned against
when we graced my mother's
best friend's family with a visit.

And, of course, there was grandma,
our matriarchal Buddha,
God's own *made* lady
perched in a front row pew
doling out prayers like parcels
of pity on her single party line
direct to the Almighty.

She was ours.

Property is private.

They owned the problems.

We owned the solutions.

That's what I believed
about my family and their family—
the family of my mother's best friend—
a half century ago.

Today
I sit at the feet of my mother's best friend:
90 going on 70,
husband long dead,
children folding her
like an origami flower
into the fabric of their lives

she owns the answers
to the questions I did not know
how to ask then
and refuse to burden her with now.

She laughs,
the correct answer to all questions unasked.

I miss your mom, she says,
she was my best friend.

A Couple of Weeks After Her Husband Died

Before she begins she pours
a scotch with just a splash
and sits at the kitchen table.

Before she begins she cradles her forehead
in the heels of her hands and thinks
it never ends as we wish:

*the final exhalation   held
the sinking   the sinking
into downy white silence.*

She pushes away from the table
opens the closet door once again:
box of shoes and boots in the corner
jumble of scarves and gloves and mittens
on the shelf—jackets coats sweaters
hanging on decisions that must be made
                              must be made . . .

She reaches in
pulls out the old tennis racket
considers the swing she doesn't take
blindly at this life   this damn life

returns the racket to its borrowed space
touches a sweater sleeve
shuts the door and begins

the journey back up the stairs
skipping the middle tread with a squeak
taking wide berth around
the leg   his leg
(the one he strapped on in the mornings
the one the grandkids snuck upstairs to stare at)
still leaning against the post at the foot of the bed.

At the Parkinson's Support Group Meeting

A slight woman with short gray hair
and small red mouth
pecking at words
like a finger at a typewriter,

tells me,
*Oh, that was in the Overeaters Anonymous
chapter of my life,
now I'm in the Parkinson's chapter.*

I wished to ask her the names
of the other chapters in her life
but it was getting late
and I didn't know her well.

Later, at home, in the kitchen,
I finish my drink, turn off the kitchen light,
move blindly through dark rooms
to get to where I, too, must go.

After the Facts

My neighbor Mitch has been talking about selling
for several years now. His wife died around five years ago
when she fell asleep at the wheel, was awoken,
then put back to sleep by a big oak. Our lots are big too
so I didn't learn about his wife until six months after the fact
when the daffodils arrived and we reacquainted ourselves
with the sun and the line at the edge of our lots.
Mitch's forearms and elbows are distorted with odd-shaped
tumor-like bulges, though they may be misplaced
pockets of muscle from 40 years hacking and hauling
choice cuts of beef from the sides of steer.
The pool he put in a couple of years before
his wife died to lure the grandkids over to the house
now features a layer of green scum, minus the grandkids.
The deck is falling apart and his lawn, never sullied by a dandelion
when his wife was alive, is now carpeted with thick green spikes
sharper than a butcher's blade. Mitch had a girlfriend
a couple years back. My wife and I ran into them
at a local restaurant. They were holding hands but it seems his grip
wasn't tight enough because she's since slipped away.
Yes, Mitch is talking about selling.
I saw him driving down the street today in the old Mercury,
slumped a little lower in the seat, steering wheel a little bit bigger,
as if that big old Mercury might soon be driving itself—which
made me think of Dad, who died back in '93.
Toward the end, one day when I visited him at the nursing home
and noticed the empty bed on the other side of the room,
I asked him what happened to his *neighbor*—Henry . . . Hank . . .
can't remember now who was lying there the day before—
and Dad said, "Oh, he died last night," then went on to tell me
what they were serving for lunch.

Attraction and Resistance

Didn't see him much when his dad was living there
but now that the house is up for sale
(Dad tumbling off the wagon, Mom five years gone)
he's there a couple of times a week

mowing the lawn, fiddling with the flower beds,
preparing it for strangers and their better days ahead.
On the weekends he and his adolescent daughter
ride ATVs in eccentric orbits around the house.
Ponytail flapping, she circles

like a satellite. In short staccato bursts,
he presses from behind,
measuring the long view,
remembering what wishes to be forgotten,
calculating distance, velocity, inclination,
resisting gravity's pull.

Mother's Sitcom Wisdom

Picture
the tagalong kid,
little brother who'll surely find
a frog to bother or puddle to play in
while older brother and father
dangle lines in the river, perform
the serious and tedious work of bonding.

Picture
little brother pleased and proud
to hold big brother's pole
when he gets up to pee,
nearly peeing himself
when bobber dips, cane pole jerks
and up pops a three-inch bluegill
flopping and wriggling
on the weed-tufted shore.

Picture
little brother afterthought,
excited as a river burble
that he's snagged the big one,
the only one, sadly
as it turns out,
right through the eye—
mistake, miscalculation,
like spilling milk
at the dinner table,
no call for decapitation/cannibalization,
he reasons, they say whines,

then acquiesce,
out of weariness, not mercy—
quit your crying and keep the damn fish
(big brother thinking)
let her make the decision, read last rites,
(Dad grumbling to himself)—
which she does, standing in the kitchen
staring into the milky gaze
of a one-eyed blue gill
while considering
Aunt Bee's no-nonsense advice
Donna Stone's empathetic kindness
(Lucy no help here)
all of whom she's been studying
on the 19-inch RCA for several years now,

before commanding
scat now, wash your hands,
for you, only you,
on your fork then in your tummy,
with you, only you,
forever.

When Yes Means No

Father's response generally *no*
I always asked Mother first.

Nerves, she'd whisper,
never the same after the war.

I didn't care,
just wanted to hear
the ping ding *yes*
of pocket change
to pay for
the jingle jangle tunes
spewing from the ice cream truck
creeping down the street.

Years later
at the nursing home
Father cupped
Mother's imprisoned face
in the palms of his hands
and repeated *yes yes yes*
over and over
for fifteen years—
until she finally quit
the argument

and I finally understood
that this *yes*
was his way
another way
a better way
to say *no.*

Deduction

The scientist says Ardi,
short for Ardipithecus,
our 4.4-million-year-old ancestor,
probably traded copulation for food.

Ardi, sexy little Ardi,
our Pliocenic Babs—
never quite sure just how
they deduce these hypothetical presumptions
from a pile of dusty old bones.

But deduce is what we do.
Perhaps this scientist, when he was a child,
deduced that he could seduce
the little girl next door with a piece of candy
and discovered his clinical bones
so to speak
playing doctor in a musty old closet.

Not an unreasonable deduction:
My brother as an adolescent
would tilt the lampshade
so the light shined on his face just right
and ten years later
was announcing the news.

Mother, as a young housewife,
sat at the piano playing *Love Is a Many-Splendored Thing*
over and over while staring at a blank wall
and a couple of decades later was talking gibberish
to the nursing home walls.

I, as a child,
snuck off to the woods,
crawled into the undergrowth,
covered myself with leaves

and here I am, a half century later, thinking
Little Ardi should have picked her own bananas,
wishing Mother would have played another song.

Choices

If

Columbus had landed in California
instead of the Bahamas,
the Pilgrims, say, in San Diego
instead of Plymouth,
Conestogas might have sailed
east on westerlies,
I might be living in the Mideast
rather than the Midwest,
Manifest Destiny
greeted what rises
rather than chasing
what sets

mood

traveling just above
latitudes of mercy

tears the treasure
smiles the lies

the furry creatures
offer their purring comforts

to ease the arguments
of the day   the age

with whom
do we make the appointment

when hope devolves into fingers
tangled in fur?

The Hard Earth

into which he pounds his stake
like a carpenter his nail
neither gives   nor forgives:

home   nylon dome
stuffed grocery cart
parked on sidewalk curb

electric blue tarp hiding
a city's debris/a human's treasure
accuses. Slump-shouldered

Buddha on the concrete corner
holds up his cardboard sign
"There but by the grace . . ." you know the rest

his only job and most difficult one it is
to capture an eye   divert a gaze
interrupt the rhythms

of denial and shame
before the light turns green
and we hurry home.

Tuning In, Tuning Out

The TV pundit knows his audience needs a moment of levity
to stay tuned to the gravity of his diatribes:

so, he gives us, the conservative congressman,
cloak fallen, party animal exposed,
caught skinny dipping in the Sea of Galilee—
the exact same spot, our pundit presumes,
where Jesus walked on water.

I take my own walk through the house:
there's the dishes, floor to scrub, dog could use a bath—
soap and water seem to be the theme here, I think,
just as the TV shouts, *Theft of Tide Rampant
Throughout the US.*

I run for cover to avoid details
that might ruin the headline.
Because right now, this moment,
I've flushed—I mean fleshed—
the whole thing out:

The entire nation, TVs blaring,
container of contraband Tide in hand,
wandering through rooms eying
dishes, dogs, floors, clothes, souls
searching for something—anything—
to clean.

Here's the News

The cable newswoman is bothering me
a bit, I must admit. Her lovely visage
crowned in high-def glory
with a perfectly coiffed head of red
is heartbreakingly beautiful.

But I can't keep my eyes off her throat—
the way all that vocal apparatus pushes
and protrudes and, yes, precludes
the possibility that beauty might be heeded
and the mute button not needed.

Game-Break Quiz

When the kids were young
and the game-break commercials came on
I'd offer my critique.
What's that mean? I'd ask.
Just be? Just be what? What
do I need to be?
Buy it? What? That?
Will I be that
if I buy it? What is it?
Tell me what it is
I should buy to be
it or that? It looks like
a single quote that's lost its footing,
I'd offer up for discussion.
Or maybe a spermatozoon
taking a nap, I'd think to myself.
Just leave us be and go pee
like normal people do
when a touchdown is scored
and extra point made,
they chimed,
leave the its and thats to us,
for now we will be
what they wish us to be
then one day we too
will get up to pee.

Gin & Tonic Afternoon

above this wind shorn
gin & tonic afternoon
the maple tosses its leafy arms
in lament or praise
my choice   here
on the front porch rocking
in a wooden chair purchased twenty years ago
from a blind man whose preternatural fingers
caressed the roof rails of my car
strategizing the nest he might build
the knots he might tie
to move this chair safely
from Kentucky to Wisconsin
where it might one day hold a man
sipping gin & tonic
determining a tree's intentions

Big Boats, Backyard Bunkers and the Next Big Bang

Perhaps I shouldn't judge
but when some guy
with more money
and more time than I
has a bad dream
involving a lot of water
so builds an ark
to prove once and for all
that man and his minions,
(aka women and beasts here)
could have been saved,
and thus, by a curious leap of logic
whereby the conditional becomes factual,
were saved
by way of a 95-foot-wide x 410-foot-long x 75-foot-tall
five-story Yahweh-designed yacht
as specced out in Genesis 6:15,
I do get a bit leery and weary,
though, all things considered,
it might make more eschatological sense
and is considerably more ambitious
than crouching ostrich like
beneath a desk
fingers laced over the back of your head,
or diving into a backyard bunker
to fork down canned peaches
and stewed tomatoes
while waiting for the next big bang
to signal world's end
so we can begin again,
which sadly we seem to do—
wait, keep waiting
for the end
to begin
again.

Death of Metaphor
(or listening to the news while gazing out the window)

The big maple's limbs groan
open and shut
like jaws taking bites
out of a frightened cloud.

On the news
a blade drops   head falls
or
blade falls   head drops.

Either is that.

How medieval   how modern
how nothing less
or more

than a razor-sharp crease
exposed
when the collar is turned back

demarcation
separating breath
from death

21st century *is*
what it is truncation of
life   language

branches swaying
clouds drifting by.

Words in the Mouth of the One
Who Refuses to Speak

According to that cynical little emperor
with the congenital itch on his chest,
religion keeps the poor from murdering the rich.
But times change and today,
in the Year of My Son and Your Lord 2017,
there's no reason to discriminate between
the haves and have-nots on the killing fields
of the righteous. Witness those earnest little guys and gals
with a death wish strapped to their bellies hell bent
to explode through the pearly gates.
Reading a little too much Joshua, anyone?
As if I, the Omniscient One,
haven't considered My own homeland security.
And those eschatological morons delivering in exegetic frenzy
what they wrote and say I said—
they make Me yawn.
I've tried to make it clear that Me and He
arrived at Our compromises eons ago.
That wild Russian got it right: My Son offered
radical freedom (though I must say, given your Old
Testament behaviors, with a measure of parental trepidation
on My part) and the Crafty One smiled craftily
and said, *Yes, I'll give them that.*
Forgive My Son, He was young and a bit naïve;
He believed in you, called it modeling behavior
though no one was paying attention.
Sure, that Trickster took advantage of the situation
what with My Son in the depths of depression, enjoining Him
go ahead, step off into the abyss and be saved.
But My Son refused the bait, said,
No   I am   the Son of Man,

traded his Immaculate Birthright
to preserve the reputation of His Father,
and freedom of humankind.
Oh, that wily Son of a Bitch—
that's why I threw Him out of paradise
way back when: He understood Adam
better than I did. And Eve—
it's difficult to influence an afterthought.
But Me and Him—We've come to terms.
We've each got Our talents and agendas.
Besides, you can only stay angry so long,
though those Mideastern dolts may prove Me wrong.
Hear Me:
without that Dark Angel, you verily
would be left to your own self-destructive devices
with no one but yourselves to blame.
As they say, everyone needs someone to hate—
you're welcome.
Truth is, I've run out of tales to tell.
I'm confounded by your answers
to the questions you fail to ask.
I'm tired. One day off a week
seems hardly enough.
Yes, pour me a glass of wine—*merci.*
Blood of My Son sacrificed for you—*de nada.*
Oh, before I forget, that little emperor—
those portraits should show him with his hand in his pants
because that's where it was when no one was looking.

Resolution

When does one exit the quarrel? Cynics vote
death. I choose today, a day of labor—
pressure washer and backyard deck, rote
stains washed away, torpor-

tinged habits rinsed clean, like old viscous oils
rendered, released of pretense
and mucilaginous ways, the toil
of flow chart arrows pointing here . . . there . . . hence

nowhere. The body's labor now the body's reward.
And later, served on a platter,
a cold beer toasting a sinking sun poured
into molten clouds illuminating what matters:

The shade beneath
this ring of trees wound into an earthly wreath.

New Year

so this is the New Year
that personal solstice

tenuous thread
binding history to hope

promises wished
into the blue black night

easily forgotten
in the day's dull light

outside
on the nearly empty feeder

an irascible jay squanders seed
onto the gray frozen earth

his bad humor
a squirrel's good fortune

I have noticed and now vow
to remember

Mantra

winter clouds lift   spring
another turn of the wheel

here rhododendrons burst
again   blood red

what is repeated is memorized
what is memorized is repeated

winter clouds lift   spring
another turn of the wheel

On Being and Becoming

Shall I strive to be
better than I am?
More than I am?

And if I become better
or more, will I become
other than who I am?

Halted and humbled,
in this illusive moment
called now

to which
history lays claim
and tomorrow aspires,

I turn my cheek
to time's callous and cruel intentions,
raise my glass in communality

and fall
with you
into who we are.

About the Author

Robert Nordstrom was raised in Ohio, where as a child he climbed trees in suburbia searching for a way up and out. After a stint in Viet Nam, a number of years sweating in front of restaurant kitchen broilers, a year in Paris with his wife Linda, he finally found his way to Wisconsin where he lived for 40 years until he and his wife moved to Oregon to be closer to children and grandchildren.

For over 30 years he worked as an editor and writer for various trade and scholarly publications and taught writing at the university level. After retiring he drove a school bus for several years teaching high schoolers how to respond when an adult says good morning and kindergarteners that it's probably best they not lick the seat in front of them.

Nordstrom's poetry, essays and fiction have appeared in numerous national and regional literary publications. His poetry has received awards from the Wisconsin Fellowship of Poets and the Oregon Poetry Association. His poem "Old Lovers" won the 2014 Hal Prize, and his 2015 collection *The Sacred Monotony of Breath* garnered an award from the Council for Wisconsin Writers.

www.ingramcontent.com/pod-product-compliance
Lightning Source LLC
Chambersburg PA
CBHW022015160426
43197CB00007B/439